DOURO VALLEY

JOURNEYS AND STORIES

pedro veloso / susana fonseca / sérgio fonseca

OBJECTO ANÓNIMO

Douro. A monumental landscape, a combined work of man and nature. Here, the local communities have adapted to the specific conditions of the territory, in many aspects hostile to life, transforming them into survival factors. Over the millennia, those communities have developed ways of settlement, relations' systems and economic activities which overcame the natural constraints and integrated them into a cultural microcosm, focused on vineyard cultivation, wine production and its transportation to distant markets. As Aquilino Ribeiro wrote, "... the Douro region, considered as an environment, is a wonder of man, not a wonder of creation. Every single thing there sings of the strength and victory of its settlers. From the stone, the earth was made, from the fierce sun, the generous liqueur, which has an aftertaste of ember and raspberries".

The wine-growing shell that goes along about one hundred kilometres of the River Douro course, in the Northern Portugal inland region, from the granite foothills of Marão and Montemuro, to the International Douro cliffs, offers exceptional conditions for the vineyard cultivation, despite the hardness of the work and the low productivity, only compensated by the excellence and distinctiveness of its wines. On the steep slopes of River Douro and its tributaries, with stony schist soils and protected from the humid winds of the Atlantic and the cold winds of Meseta, an "evolving and living cultural landscape" was formed, acknowledged by UNESCO as World Heritage. Such acknowledgement consecrated precisely the importance of the Douro region in the world wine-growing overview, not only as a production area of one of the most prestigious wines on a global scale, the Port wine, but most of all as a cultural heritage, defined by the historical depth of the secular relation process between man and nature.

Furthermore, the Douro Demarcated Region is one of the oldest and largest historical wine-growing regions in the world, covering about 250 thousand hectares. From among mountainous wine-growing regions, it is the largest and most historically significant one, with the longest continuity and the biggest biological diversity of the grape varieties here perfected. Upper Douro is, therefore, a remarkable example of a landscape which illustrates the different stages of human history. To cultivate vineyards on the slopes of River Douro and its tributaries, man had to produce soil and built terraces, traditionally supported by schist walls and, more recently, by vineyard specific ways of arrangement, suitable for mechanisation. Today, the Douro wine-growing landscape constitutes a complex and dynamic architecture that pays witness to the continued work of transforming the mountains into "hanging gardens", according to the well-known term by Jaime Cortesão. From Barqueiros to Mazouco, across the whole Douro wine-growing Region, it can be perceived a traditional wine-growing culture, which marked and continues to mark knowledge and gestures, memories and sensibilities, rhythms and calendars, lifetime pictures and relations' systems.

But the focus on the wine-growing culture - the construction and reconstruction of the regional landscape, at the pace of the developing techniques, as well as of the economic and institutional policies which made Douro, since two and a half centuries ago, the first demarcated and regulated wine-growing region in the world - has not extinguished the identity power of the natural elements. Nor of the narrow river that runs between mountains, despite the hydroelectric dams system which tamed its uneven course. Of the poor and stony soils of the schist slopes. Of a Mediterranean environment, which is felt in the aroma of the autochthonous vegetation, in the warm and dry microclimate of the wine-growing valley, which contrasts with the one from the cold surrounding land, and in the ecosystems that best resisted to the actions of man.

The Douro, Miguel Torga wrote, is "the wonder of a landscape that stops being it due to the risk of overmeasuring itself. It is not a panorama that the eyes contemplate: it is an excess of nature. [...] A geological poem. The absolute beauty.".

Vineyards only occupy about 45 thousand hectares, less than 20% of this territory. It is often associated with other Mediterranean-type cultures, such as the olive tree or the almond tree grove, mainly in Upper Douro. Here and there, on the protected valleys, orange trees grow. And other fruit trees, from the famous cherry trees of Penajóia, Resende or Alfândega da Fé, to the apple trees, peach trees or apricot trees, especially in South Douro. And the traditional fig trees, all over the place, even if the economic exploitation of the celebrated Douro dried figs is now less important than in the past. And vegetable-gardens, where home-grown products achieve treasured flavours. However, a large part of the Douro territory is not cultivated. In some lands agricultural activity is unlikely to be found, especially in granite outcropping regions of Marão, Cachão and International Douro, in mountainous transition areas, or in certain steeper paths through the valleys of the tributaries. The obsession with the wine-growing has devalued those areas of woods and Mediterranean forests, where the native flora resists with remarkable vivacity. Strawberry trees, cork oak trees, junipers, terebinths, grain trees, deciduous oak trees and other tree species are combined, here and there, with numerous varieties of shrubs and brushwood, where predominate the rock roses, heathers, gorses, rosemaries, brooms, common rues, silver nailroot and many others. The intensity of colours, aromas and environments, the rarity of certain species and the importance some of them play on the local ecological balance, contributing for the survival of wild fauna, constitute irreplaceable values. Hunting species, such as the wild boar, the wild rabbit, the hare, the partridge and others. But also several bird species, some of them facing extinction, such as the griffon vulture, the golden eagle, Bonelli's eagle, the vulture, the stork, the eagle owl, the black wheatear (which Tait called "the Port-wine bird"), the falcon, the jay, the crow, the heron, etc. Or even the roe deer, the fox, the wildcat, more rarely the wolf, and many other wild mammals species. And numerous varieties of reptiles, as well as piscicultural and amphibian species, such as the otter.

However, Upper Douro is far from being a homogenous area. Admittedly, from a natural point of view, some elements tend towards a regional identification: the river, the uneven terrain, the predominance of schist, the environment Mediterranean features. It is also true that, seen over the long term, the history of this territory allows us to perceive some identity civilizational characteristics. The opening to an exchange of diverse cultural influences has formed, since the most distant times, a region of cultural syncretism, whether in the collective traditional imaginary (expressed, for example, in legends, sometimes mixing the Arab myth with aspects of the Celtic and Christian imaginary), or in the multiple archaeological vestiges of human settlement, some of them dating back to the prehistoric period, from which it stands out the "sanctuary" of Palaeolithic rock art of the Coa Valley, even though expressed in many other testimonies somewhat scattered throughout the region. And, above all, the centrality of a wine-growing culture with strong historical roots, dating back at least to the Roman period and which, over the last three centuries, by projecting itself abroad, has been established as a dominating integrating element of a large part of the valley, in economic, social and symbolic terms. However, these unifying elements of the Douro region do not extinguish its valuable diversity heritage. Natural and cultural one. From Barqueiros to the border, the variations are evident. One can easily feel the contrast between the mountain and the river, between the sunnier north bank and the south bank, between Upper Douro, Cima Corgo and Baixo Corgo. It is not difficult to sense flagrant differences, sometimes in the same parish just a few kilometres away, from the river bank to the top of the mountains. The uneven terrain, cut by numerous rivers and mountain streams, some of them dry in the summer and torrential in the winter, generates an enormous diversity of environments, colours, sensations, as well as different conditions of human settlement and land exploitation, a mosaic of landscape units, with similar motifs, but which never repeat themselves.

As one goes east up the River Douro, the climate, the landscape, the economy, the settlements, the customs, and even the way people talk, it all changes. Until Cachão da Valeira, in its traditional area, with vineyards dominating the landscape. Beyond Tua, in Upper Douro, only considered part of the demarcated region in the 20th century, olive and almond tree groves compete for the land against the vineyards. As we approach the border, the heat and the dryness of the summer increase, as do the temperature variations. Less densely occupied and with concentrated settlements, the landscape is less humanized. At each step, there are steep slopes of bare schist, "ungrateful land, where the heather struggles to bloom", as wrote the poet Guerra Junqueiro. Only rarely does the landscape widen into fertile plains, uncovering orchards or vegetable-gardens. Vilariça is an exception, with its widen flood plains. In all Upper Douro, despite the expansion of the vine, the ex libris continues to be the spectacle of the blossoming almond trees, by the end of winter.

It is also worth to go on through the valleys of the River Douro tributaries. Varosa, Corgo, Ceira, Távora, Tedo, Torto, Pinhão, Tua, Teja, Sabor, Côa, Águeda, Mosteiro. The heart of the Douro beats within all of them, to which they run to, defined by the identity features of the region. And, nevertheless, all of them differentiate from each other, with specific ecosystems, diverse landscapes, vestiges of ancient settlements, a fabulous intangible heritage. Douro is all this, diverse and indivisible... Of nature and of man, as wrote the poet Pires Cabral: "And we are that river, made of a thousand rivers and streams, and that mountain, made of a thousand mountains and hills. We just need eyes to see it. The river: the rustling and fragile water. The mountain: the steady and severe stone".

PORTO

D. LUÍS I BRIDGE

Side by side with the River Douro, Porto city has an area of 26 ml², where today live about 240 thousand people. If we add the adjacent municipalities to it, we find the limits of the great metropolitan area of Porto, with approximately one and a half million inhabitants.

With very remote origins, the city was named Portus, located on the opposite side of the Cale village, at the other bank of the River Douro, later asserting itself as the main city of County of Portugal, or Portucale (territory which gave origin to the name of the country).

It played a prominent role at the beginning of the Portuguese Discoveries and received the designation of Cidade Invicta - today still called that way - by the time of the liberal wars.

Porto is also known by its famous Port Wine, by its historical centre, classified as World Heritage by UNESCO, and by its football team (Futebol Clube do Porto).

The city boasts many sights, of which the "Torre dos Clérigos" (Clérigos Tower), designed by Nasoni, and the Serralves Foundation, with its Museum of Contemporary Art are of particular interest. The Historical Quarter is World Heritage, classified by UNESCO. Foz is another highly touristic area, considered by many to be the prettiest area of the city, where the beauty of the sea, the beaches and esplanades can be enjoyed, together with the beautiful and romantic areas for seaside trips. Today, the city of Porto welcomes more than a million tourists per year.

PAGE 9 → (from up to the right)

01-RABELO BOAT, NEAR PORTO'S RIBEIRA

02- PORTO'S CATHEDRAL

03- CLÉRIGOS TOWER

04- RIBEIRA

ARABIAN ROOM AT PALÁCIO DA BOLSA

PRAÇA DA LIBERDADE (SQUARE) AND AVENIDA DOS ALIADOS (AVENUE)

SERRALVES MUSEUM OF CONTEMPORARY ART

SERRALVES HOUSE

CASA DA MÚSICA

PORT WINE

RABELO BOAT

Port Wine is considered a symbol of Portugal all over the world. Who never tried a glass of this precious nectar on special occasions? This wine contains the history of a region and its people that over the years became a collective cultural heritage of work and experiences. This splendid nectar is connected since its conception to the Douro Demarcated Region, but the cellars also play their part in the final result of this product, as it is here that the wine is stored, aged and sold. Many of these cellars offer you the chance to get to know the entire Port Wine process. At the end you might also be invited to taste a glass of Port.

The Rabelo is a Portuguese vessel typical of the River Douro that was used to transport oak casks of Port Wine from Upper Douro to Vila Nova de Gaia, where the wine was stored and sold. It is a mountain river boat with 21 to 25 yards long. Its design bears similarities to the Nordic vessels, and others of a similar Mediterranean style. With a square sail, the Rabelo was normally crewed by six or seven men. The river transport guaranteed by the rabelos went into decline since the 19th century with the development of other means of transportation. Nowadays, they are a tourist attraction on the River Douro.

PORT WINE CELLARS

PORT WINE

Port Wine is unquestionably one of Portugal's strong symbols around the world. The origins of its name come from the city of Porto (Oporto), from where it was exported from the river port.

Until the 17th century, the red wine from the Douro region was described as being too full-bodied and, for many, as having a bitter taste. In the 17th century, wars and rivalries among the Northern European kingdoms ended up promoting the Portuguese wine rather than the famous French wines. The trade stabilisation between Portugal and England brought by the Methuen Treaty in 1703 welcomed Port Wine to the British homes, leading to a growth on exports. In order to protect its name, quality and production, a company was created to control all activities relating to Port Wine, thus giving birth to what nowadays is the world's oldest demarcated and regulated wine region!

The demarcated wine region covers an area of 26 thousand hectares and was classified by UNESCO a World Heritage Site in 2001, referred to as Região Vinhateira do Alto Douro. Nowadays it is one of the most popular tourism regions in Portugal.

Port Wine still has a significant role on exports, which contributes to the promotion of Portugal abroad.

→ *(FROM LEFT TO THE RIGHT)*
PORTO WINE TAWNY, RUBY AND WHITE

Varieties

Any Port Wine variety is perfect to raise your glass and celebrate with your friends or family. One can say that there is a Port Wine suitable for every taste, as there is a wide range of varieties, both red and white, although the latter is not as famous worldwide. These are the most common varieties:

Vintage: Vintage is a wine of excellence which comes from a single harvest. Vintage wines are declared as such only in years of exceptional quality. The wine is aged in oak casks for a maximum of 3 years and then in the bottle for a period of up to 40 years. This wine is not filtered when bottled so, when opened, it should be consumed within 48 hours, as the wine will quickly oxidize.

LBV: Late Bottled Vintage Ports are similar in appearance to Ruby red wines, and are made from one single harvest of very high quality. Before being bottled they mature in oak barrels for 4 to 6 years. LBV wines can be consumed immediately after being bottled or mature inside the bottle.

Ruby: This wine is similar in colour to a ruby gemstone, since during the ageing process little or no oxidisation takes place (usually up to 3 years in oak casks). It is a young full-bodied wine, with a strong flavour and rich red berry aromas.

Tawny: These wines are obtained from blends of various batches of Port aged in vats or oak casks, which leads to a colour evolution. Over time the strong ruby colour is lost and slowly mellows into a golden-brown colour. It has aromas of dried fruits and wood. The varieties are: Tawny, Tawny Reserve, Tawny with age indication (10, 20, 30 and 40 years) and Colheita (Portuguese for "harvest"). These are blends of batches of various ages, except for the Colheita, which is similar to a Tawny with age indication made from batches aged during the same amount of time.

White: White Port is the only one categorised by its sweetness, which results from the way the wine is produced. The varieties are: dry white, light dry white and sweet – also known as Lágrima (Portuguese for "tear"). White Port wines have lower alcohol content, not below 16,5% by volume. White Port wines have lower alcohol content with a minimum of 16.5°.

15

HISTORY OF DEMARCATED REGION OF DOURO

MARQUÊS DE POMBAL (MARQUIS OF POMBAL)

Sebastião José de Carvalho e Melo was born in Lisbon in 1699. He received the titles of Count of Oeiras and Marquis of Pombal, and his efforts regarding the Douro Wine-growing Region represented the major driving force of this area, with the creation, in 1756, of the Companhia Geral da Agricultura das Vinhas do Alto Douro, a company directed for the production and distribution of this region's wines. He was a Minister under King José I kingdom and ruled the country for a long period until the King's death, doing so with great authority, sometimes even in a despotic manner. He carried out great economic, social, political and cultural reforms and the reconstruction of the city of Lisbon, after the earthquake in 1755. Many other important measures took place under his supervision, such as the reform of the University of Coimbra.

His efforts to create the Douro Demarcated Wine-growing Region were aimed at protecting the wine quality, preventing counterfeit wine to be produced and inserted on the region, thus protecting the Port Wine business on the English market. This decision was badly taken by the English but, nevertheless, it was established what is now the oldest Demarcated and Regulated Wine-growing Region in the world.

BARÃO DE FORRESTER (BARON OF FORRESTER)

Joseph James Forrester was born in England in 1809. Nephew of a wealthy Port Wine merchant, he came to the city of Porto very young, and soon fell in love with the river and the Douro region. His passion was such that he ordered the construction of a luxurious and refined boat. A covered Rabelo, exclusively built for him to be able to spend long seasons on the river and to take his friends to his house at Ramada Alta, where he would serve exquisite banquets. He wrote and painted about Porto and Douro, and meticulously mapped the river on a 118 x 27" map. This work earned him the title of Baron of Forrester, awarded by the Portuguese King. He died in 1861, in consequence of an accident with D.ª Antónia's boat when passing by Cachão da Valeira.

DOURO'S MAP, MADE BY THE BARON OF FORRESTER

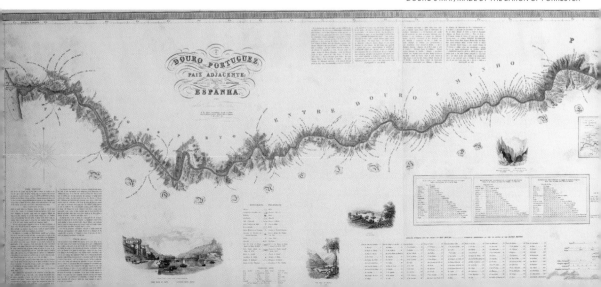

DONA ANTÓNIA ADELAIDE FERREIRA

D.ª Antónia Adelaide Ferreira was one of the most important personalities in the history of Douro and Port Wine. A courageous and determined woman, daughter of a rich landowner and wine merchant, born in Régua in 1811. Her work made her one of the great investors behind the Port Wine business. She bought important farms, renovated many of them and established the Vale do Meão farm, by ordering the construction of warehouses, starting major vineyard plantings and carrying out improvement works, especially during times of crisis in the region, when some vine diseases (powdery mildew and phylloxera) occurred.

With the importance D.ª Antónia Ferreira acquired in the country, the Duke of Saldanha, at the time head of the government, wanted his son to marry with D.ª Antónia's daughter, but she refused. The Duke of Saldanha then planned to kidnap her 12-year-old daughter, although there is no evidence that he was, in fact, involved. When D.ª Antónia found out about this situation, she left for England, where she stayed until 1856.

When the levels of wine production were really high and the producers could not sell all of it, D.ª Antónia purchased vast amounts of wine to prevent prices from falling. As she was a brilliant businesswoman, she managed to sell the majority of the production to England. She died in 1896, at age 85, in Quinta das Nogueiras.

DEMARCATED REGION OF DOURO

The wine production in Douro has existed since pre-Roman times, but only in 1756, by the Royal Charter of King José I, did Douro become a demarcated and regulated wine-growing region, being, at present time, the oldest in the world. This region has a total area of 250000 ha, 24000 of them classified by UNESCO as World Heritage, where there are over 30000 wine-growers.

Douro Wine-growing Region is naturally divided into three main areas, distinct in geography and climate. Baixo Corgo is located downstream of River Corgo, which is a tributary of Douro River, and it has an Atlantic Mediterranean climate, with temperate summers and winters, greater rainfall and more fertile land. Cima Corgo, between the rivers Corgo and Tua, is a region of transition, with higher temperature variations, deeper valleys and steeper mountains. Upper Douro, located upstream of Tua up to the border with Spain, is a region where the summers are extreme, the winters quite cold and the rainfall lower, which makes the land drier and hotter.

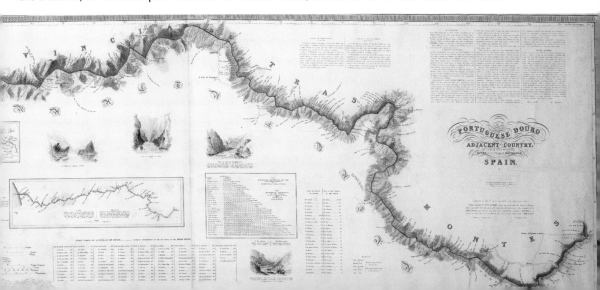

1 . CORRÊA RIBEIRO & FILHOS (MONTE CARLO) | 2. SOC. DOS VINHOS DO PORTO (MARUJO)
3. PORT WINE DOMINGOS GONÇALVES DE SÁ & FILHOS (VELHINHO) | 4. PORT WINE PINHO & CABRAL (PORTO-BIZARRO)
PAGE 19 5 . SANDEMAN'S PORT (LOXTON KNIGHT) | 6. RAMOS-PINTO - "THE KISS", BY RENÉ VICENT
7. SANDEMAN'S PORT (DANCING WOMEN, JEAN D'YLEN) | 8. PORT WINE AMADEU

5

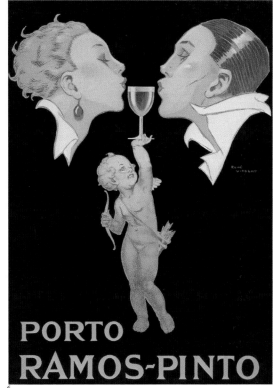

6

7

8

$\mathcal{I}$ arrived in this country of *saudade* with an almost empty backpack. I checked-in, followed a path of agitated clouds, left the sweat of work marked on a grey seat and followed the direction, as planned, along a waterway to the *Douro Valley* I had heard about. I was curious about what I would find, since a couple of friends came to this region so often and repeated so many times that I too should come here.

One day, after leaving the alarm on, I made my way to work, as always. I saw all my e-mails and booked my trip with an online agency.

Now that I heard the guide's descriptions of the oldest demarcated and regulated wine-growing region in the world, I felt much lighter, absorbing more and more the green landscape mixed with gold.

I arrived here reinvigorated, I see myself reflected in the faces of the smiling children who run after their mothers,

The Embrace of the Sun

despite the hot air that invited them to rest. I lean back into a shadow to listen to the sources of light shining on the earth and the shale, making it ideal to receive the product of the arduous work of these people that seem to know how to live in a profound calm, without any thought to torment them, although a more attentive look will notice that it isn't quite like that. The concerns are also there, within the most loaded stares.

And I still have a lot to do and visit during this trip. In my notepad, there are some places not to be missed, recommended by my friends: a visit to a farm to try the nectar that is produced here, a trip on a historical train, a visit to the village of Ucanha, and many other wine-growing villages that I am keen to get to know.

At this time everything seems bigger than me, and the embrace of this landscape is so tender and warm that it makes me remember by mother's embraces.

Fictional text based on a true story

CALDAS DE AREGOS

Resende is located south of River Douro. The parish of Barrô marks, to the southwest, the start of the Demarcated Wine-growing Region of Douro. The architectural heritage of the municipality is varied and rich. Examples of this are the remnants of the prehistoric period, the churches of S. Martinho de Mouros, Santa Maria de Cárquere and Barrô, all classified as National Monuments. The eighteenth-century manors, of which the Casa da Torre da Lagariça, immortalised by the writer Eça de Queiroz in his novel "The Noble House of Ramires", is of particular interest, also deserve a visit. The Caldas de Aregos Spa is an excellent location for relaxing and looking after your body. The municipality of Resende is one of the largest Portuguese producers of cherries, and the Cherry Festival can be seen at the end of May.

RIVER DOURO AT MESÃO FRIO

MAIN CHURCH OF SÃO NICOLAU

CITY COUNCIL

The first references to a village were today is located Mesão Frio date from the beginning of the 3rd century. It is known that at that time there was a hostel at the village, which was a stopping point for the travellers of the Roman Empire main routes. The interesting toponymical origin of the village is explained by the existence of that hostel, which originally helped keeping the travellers warm (mansionis frigidae).

Nowadays, Mesão Frio is part of one of the border areas of the demarcated region of Douro, surrounded by farms and vineyards over the river.

The culinary specialities that this village has to offer are shad, lamprey, trout, roasted lamb and a great variety of desserts which delights many generations.

It is a place full of history, where a visit to the Main Church of S. Nicolau and to the Convent of S. Francisco (where today is located the City Council) is recommended.

QUINTA'S MANOR-HOUSE

VIEW OVER THE RIVER DOURO

TOURIGA NATIONAL GRAPE VARIETY

Quinta do Côtto is located on the River Douro, in the municipality of Mesão Frio. It boasts an 18th century manor-house, and there are remnants of the farm that date back to the year 1140. Quinta do Côtto, which produces Douro and a Vintage Port wine, brings together old customs and new technologies and innovation in wine production, ensuring recognised quality.

On the early 60's here it was produced the first "Vinho de Quinta" of the Douro Region, which is a wine made exclusively from the grapes of a single property. Being called Vinho de Quinta, it guarantees to the final consumer that the wine was carefully produced and selected by the owner, thus ensuring its high quality.

FRENCH OAK CASKS

19TH CENTURY ROOM

Solar da Rede is a property dating from early 18th century, with a fantastic view over the River Douro and a farm with an area of 40 hectares of vine-yards and gardens. It was rebuilt and inaugurated in 1999 as an Historical Inn and became a member of Pousadas de Portugal (Inns of Portugal). The manor has 19 rooms, 8 suites and 2 luxury suites. It is worth visiting for the period decoration and architecture.

On the welcoming environment of the dining room you can enjoy some local delicacies such as "estaladiça de alheira" (bread and meat sausage), "bacalhau com cebolada" (codfish with onion) "naco de vitela" (veal) and "aletria" (sweet noodles).

Besides the magnificent landscape and the feeling of being back to the aristocratic environment that the Solar gives you through every look at the garden or at the building itself, you can even enjoy several indoor and outdoor activities, such as bird watching, bicycle rides, fishing and hiking.

MAIN VIEW OF THE MANOR-HOUSE

MONUMENT DEDICATED TO THE FARMER

CITY COUNCIL

When Santa Marta de Penaguião is mentioned, wine production and cooperation come to mind, and the best example of this is the Santa Marta Cooperative Vineyard, which is the largest cooperative organisation in the Douro region, producing much of the region's total amount of wine. Set in a verdant area totally surrounded by vineyards, the city embraces magnificent landscapes, as its various viewpoints illustrate.

STATUE REFERRING TO THE GRAPE HARVEST

LANDSCAPE WITH VINES

RÉGUA

PANORAMIC VIEW OF RÉGUA

Peso da Régua is a renowned and emblematic city of the region. With a history dating back to the Roman invasions, the city has modernized and become the centre of the Douro Railway between Porto and Pocinho.

In 1756, after the Marquis of Pombal's decision to demarcate the Douro Region, Régua became recognized as the great trading post for Port Wine. There are now various vessels that take tourists on river cruises from Régua river dock. There is a wide range of hotels and visitors can taste the regional cuisine in one of the various restaurants. One of the must-see places is the Douro Museum, whose headquarters was installed, after upgrading works, in the former Company building in 2008.

VINEYARDS AROUND THE CITY

STAINED GLASS AT CASA DO DOURO BY LINO ANTÓNIO

INNER STAIRCASE

EDUCATIONAL SERVICE BUILDING

WAREHOUSE

The main function of Douro Museum, with its Museology Service, is to create an inventory of, study and disseminate the tangible and intangible heritage of the Demarcated Douro Wine-growing Region, publicising it through the exhibitions and publications under its responsibility. It also boasts an Education Centre, which organises various activities, and an Information Centre with an archive, library and media centre. The building that is now the museum was formerly the Casa da Companhia. A restaurant and a winebar can be found inside.

SHOP

DOURO MUSEUM FAÇADE

WINE BAR

TEMPORARY EXHIBITION AREA

HOUSE OF QUINTA DO VALLADO

Quinta do Vallado, which is located very close to Régua, extends along both banks of the River Corgo. The earliest records of the farm, which was owned by D. Antónia Adelaide Ferreira during the nineteenth century, date back to 1716. It has remained in the same family for six generations. The villa produces quality Douro and Port wines, some of which have won international awards. You can walk along the banks of Corgo River, a tributary of Douro River, or even go on a canoe tour. If you prefer, you can also participate on a wine tasting, on hiking or even on a bicycle ride.

COAT OF ARMS

HOUSE OF QUINTA DA PACHECA

CELLARS

Quinta da Pacheca is one of the oldest of the Douro region. The first document which mentions it dates from 1738. It was first called "Pacheca", since the owner was Mrs Mariana Pacheco Pereira.

In 1903, Don José Freire Serpa Pinto bought the property, initiating the wine production under its own brand.

Besides the magnificent landscape, Quinta da Pacheca offers a wide range of services, including tours to the property, accommodation, wine tastings, river cruises and also a unique opportunity of making your own wine, in case you visit the Quinta at the grape harvest season. To fully enjoy the tour, end your journey with a meal prepared by Mrs Teresa Serpa Pimentel, the excellent cook of Quinta da Pacheca.

HOUSE DETAIL

SHOP

Letter I
Douro, August 6th 1915

My Dear Wife,

I hope that when you receive my lines, with which I am going to be as direct as possible, I find you in good health. I am here 'as fit as a fiddle' as they say in this country so welcoming. Our cousin wasn't exaggerating at all when he described his large properties and the arduous work that is done here to produce the wonderful wine that he usually offers us when he visits us. The mountains are populated by his vineyards planted in terraces that rise on precipices above the river. Here and there are fig trees, whose fruits I know you would greatly appreciate, and there is no lack of olive trees and picturesque farms.
At our cousin's house they maintain that mysterious habit that each guest who is sitting at the table, after dinner, must carefully pass the bottle of Port to the person on their left. It is true that this wine appears to require a special ambience, with contempt for haste and disorder.
Here, everything is matured slowly and there are sounds that hang in the ears, whichever way we turn, such as

The Embrace that Narrows Distance

the example of the unlubricated creaking wheels of cattle carts that move slowly and that can pull loads over the steep slopes, where not even a pony passes in the opposite direction. One day I tried to alert our cousin to the advantages of lubricating the wheels, but he gently explained to me that the ox only works when it hears the wheels behind it, and in addition, it is a way of warning riders who hear the sound, so that they can avoid the danger from miles away and find a safer place to pass.

I wasn't expecting to find a train around here, but despite appearing to be the slowest in the world, and passing at the most inconvenient times, our cousin appears satisfied with it. Apparently, the boatmen who used to transport spirit upstream in the rabelo boats to add to the wine used to drink a large amount of it and replace it with river water.

My dear, there is so much I have to tell you that I could write a book with it all. I shall await news from England and I will write again soon.

I anxiously await your news.

From your homesick husband, Steven Naylor

Fictional text based on a true story

GENERAL CITY OVERVIEW

SANCTUARY OF N.ª SRA. DOS REMÉDIOS

SEE OF LAMEGO

DETAIL TILES

Lamego is a monumental city, highlights of its architectural heritage being the Castle, the See and the Sanctuary and Stairway of Nossa Senhora dos Remédios. In addition to these monuments, there are various churches, houses with coat of arms, fountains and stone crosses that demonstrate the historical and religious importance that the municipality held and continues to hold over the region. Lamego was able to harmonise its history with development and the nature that surrounds it and constitutes one of the locations with a wide choice of hotels in the Douro region.

STAINED GLASS AT THE INTERIOR OF THE SANCTUARY

SANCTUARY AND STAIRWAY OF NOSSA SENHORA DOS REMÉDIOS

MAIN FAÇADE REFLECTED ON THE LAKE WITH A STATUE BY JOÃO CUTILEIRO

CELLAR, GRAPE TREADING

LIBRARY

GARDENS' DETAIL

Casa de Mateus is a baroque-style building constructed during the 18th century under the supervision of the architect Nicolau Nasoni. In 1970, the Casa de Mateus Foundation was founded with the aim of preserving the house, studying its archives and promoting cultural, scientific and educational activities. The Foundation promotes various activities such as concerts, seminars, courses and exhibitions.

At Casa de Mateus it is possible to enter its rooms, which are richly decorated and furnished in the style of the period, the chapel and the magnificent gardens, lovingly cared for. Casa de Mateus produces sweets and wine marketed by Lavradores de Feitoria.

CITY COUNCIL'S BUILDING

HOUSE OF DIOGO CÃO

PILLORY'S SQUARE

Vila Real is the district capital and was once the capital of the Trás-os-Montes province. Nowadays, one of the important focal points of the region is the University of Trás-os-Montes e Alto Douro, which attracts students to the city. The street circuit for racing cars in Vila Real is considered one of the best in Europe, and is held every year.

In the city centre, we recommend a stroll through the typical streets, where you can enjoy the regional cuisine and traditional confectionery.

Near the city, you can visit the Alvão Natural Park, where you can find the waterfalls of Fisgas of Ermelo and enjoy the plants and animals which are typical of the Park. Still in Alvão, you should visit the villages of Vila Marim and Lamas de Olo.

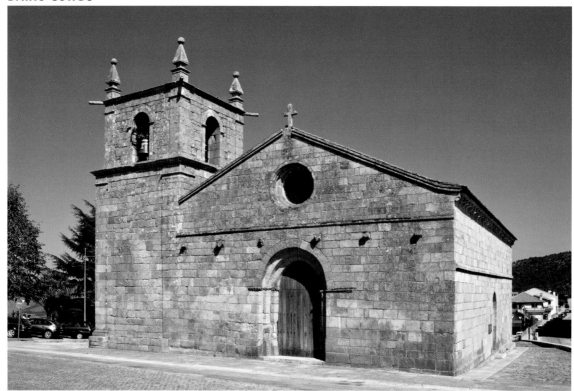

MAIN CHURCH

AGRICULTURAL PLANTING

The municipality of Armamar, with around 7000 inhabitants, shares a long border with the bed of the River Douro. Among the landscapes in the municipality, the naturally terraced slopes with their vineyards and the River Douro and its tributary, the River Tedo, are of particular importance.

As we drive south, the landscape changes dramatically, becoming typical of Beira, where the shale gives way to granite and fruit trees emerge in large quantities, mainly apple trees.

MOUTH OF TEDO RIVER

RABELO BOAT

→ *PAGES 48/49. PANORAMIC VIEW WITH PINHÃO IN THE BACKGROUND AND VENTOZELO MANOR*

Letter II
Douro, September 8th 1915

My Dear Wife,
I was delighted to hear that you are well, despite the constant rain that doesn't give any respite to the umbrellas. You must check what is happening to our cat, as it is unlikely that this loss of appetite is due to it missing its Owner. Take him to our friend Dr. Peterson for him to solve this mystery that leads our Dennis to eat less than usual.
Here it remains 'steaming hot'. Even I am beginning to miss a little refreshing rain. We are in the middle of the harvest season. The people of these lands work infinite hours, not bothering at all with what could be considered a pause for a rest. On the contrary, it appears that, in order to rid themselves of fatigue, they choose to sing and dance continuously. I myself accompany the rhythm with my feet and I have the feeling that, more than a distraction, these songs and dances appear to be an urgent need. Some of these people travel thousands of miles on foot just to participate in the festival that is the harvest.
In the vineyards there is a happy babbling that hangs constantly in the air. The women cut the bunches with long scissors or knives and separate all the defective berries before putting them into the baskets, whose grapes are after

The Embrace that Narrows Distance

transported to other larger baskets that the men carry on their heads, with enviable strength, to the press.
While babbling, the winemakers eat the delicious grapes. Our cousin says that these grapes eaten during the harvest could represent many casks of wine, but he understands that this is part of the tradition. It is a hard job, in which the greatest force comes from manual work of these men and women who are transforming the landscape and who deserve their meagre rewards. Our cousin also told me how everybody suffered with him when phylloxera destroyed much of his vineyards in 1875.
The people of the Douro face the work on the terraces as they face life, with ups and downs, with losses and gains. They know how to suffer without giving up on living. They are as one with the landscape. I also found out that these people of Douro are not only those that live here, but also those that move here from Trás-os-Montes, or even from Galicia, to help at harvest time. Today, even I feel at one with this land, but my thoughts are also with you.
I anxiously await your news.

From your homesick husband, Steven Naylor

Fictional text based on a true story

Miguel Torga is the pen name of Adolfo Correia Rocha, born in 1907 in the parish of São Martinho de Anta. He wrote poetry, essays, fiction and drama, and was one of the major Portuguese writers of the 20th century, with books translated into several languages. He qualified in Medicine, pursuing the profession in Coimbra, where he lived, but dedicated himself body and soul to writing. He left a monumental body of work, reflecting, in many of his books, Douro and its culture. He won recognized national and international literary prizes, reaching the point of being nominated for the Nobel Prize for Literature. He died in 1995 in Coimbra.

BUST IN HONOUR OF MIGUEL TORGA IN SÃO MARTINHO DE ANTA

The municipality of Sabrosa is full of cultural references that date back to prehistory, and many of its settlements originate in the Middle Ages, such as the Wine-growing Village of Provesende.

The most important personality from the municipality is the writer Miguel Torga (1907-1995), who was born in the São Martinho de Anta civil parish and has written extensively about Douro. Soon, you will be able to visit a museum dedicated to the writer in this civil parish. In Sabrosa, you can see several of the municipality's houses with coat of arms, the religious architecture and visit the House where was born Fernão de Magalhães, according to the tradition.

HOUSE AND STATUE OF THE EXPLORER FERNÃO DE MAGALHÃES

VIEW OF VINEYARDS IN SABROSA

CITY COUNCIL

WINE AGING CELLARS DESIGNED BY SIZA VIEIRA

CASA DAS PIPAS

CELLARS

Quinta do Portal is an independent Portuguese family house devoted to the production of DOC Douro, Port and Moscatel wines. It falls into the category of Quality Rural Tourism, as one may see by the comfortable and beautiful *Casa das Pipas*. Recently, Quinta do Portal invested in the construction of a new wine ageing cellar designed by architect Siza Vieira.

This wine cellar, whose main construction materials are schist and cork, allows us "to control humidity and temperature and to significantly improve the wine ageing process". Here you can enjoy several activities, from participating on the grape harvest - cutting or stepping on grapes -, taking a Douro cruise, horse riding, hiking, and much more.

              CASA DAS PIPAS, INTERIOR OF THE HOUSE

VIEW OF THE HOUSE

CHAPEL OF NOSSA SENHORA DO CARMO

HARVEST

INNER COURTYARD

With around 120 hectares of vineyards, Quinta Nova de Nossa Senhora do Carmo has been part of the Wine-growing Region of Douro since 1758. It is located near the village of Pinhão, on the north bank of the River Douro, and offers beautiful views over the river valley. This farm, which produces Douro and Port Wines, is devoted to wine tourism through its Rural Hotel and Wine House.

By visiting the Quinta, you can observe the wine making process, take a walk through the farm and its many trails, discovering historical places all over the property, or, if you want to rest and simply admire the fantastic landscape, you can enjoy the relaxing outdoor pool.

→ PÁGS. 54/55 HARVEST

HARVEST

IMAGINÁRIO DURIENSE MUSEUM

TYPICAL HOUSE

GARDEN

GENERAL VIEW OF TABUAÇO

MAIN CHURCH

Tabuaço is a small municipality located in the south of Douro. Within its territory there are remnants of the presence of various peoples since prehistoric times. This is a town closely connected to agriculture, especially wine production, with a tradition kept very much alive and present among the people. In relation to architectural heritage, the Romanesque Main Church, the various chapels spread around the municipality and the S. Pedro das Águias hermitage are of particular interest. The stunning natural landscape is also a highlight.

QUINTA DO PANASCAL

GRAPE TREADING

Dated from the 18th century, Quinta do Panascal is the most important of the three magnificent properties of Fonseca Guimaraens. Here were harvested the grapes which made Vintage Fonseca to be considered in 1994 the best wine in the world by "Wine Spectator". It also won, in 2005, the "Best of Wine Tourism" award on the "Special Wineries Tourism" category. In 2007, Quinta do Panascal was included on the top 10 most romantic spots of the European wine regions by the prestigious magazine "Decanter".

All visitors can enjoy an audio and video tour along the vineyards, during which it is described the history of the company and of its famous wines, as well a wine production process (still made in a traditional way) and a wine tasting. The Quinta has also to offer many leisure activities and a mini course of Port Wine production.

SHOP AND WINE TASTING CENTRE

GRAPE HARVEST AT THE FARM

MUST MIXTURE

INTERIOR OF THE HOUSE

QUINTA DO SEIXO

SHOP

PORT WINE

It is with a fabulous view over the Douro River that we are welcomed to this property, which has received the "New Private Project" award by Turismo de Portugal.

Inaugurated in September 2007 with the visit of the European Union Agriculture Ministers, Quinta do Seixo has available several kinds of tours: Classic (the most economical one), Vau Vintage, Wine Bar and Gourmet. There is also the opportunity to enjoy picnics or even wine workshops.

All production is destined to Sandeman, a company known all over the world by the quality of its wines as well as for "Sandeman Don", an image incorporated on the company's advertising campaigns and labels since 1930, being internationally recognised as a symbol of prestige and quality.

VIEW FROM THE FARM

TASTING ROOM

MAIN CHURCH

SANFINS DO DOURO

STATUE IN HONOUR OF THE MAN OF THE DOURO

Alijó is one of the municipalities with the strongest link to vineyard culture and enjoys beautiful landscapes and slopes dropping off to the River Douro, Tua and Pinhão. The Casal de Loivos viewpoint has already been considered by a British newspaper as the third most beautiful view in the world. The Rivers Douro, Pinhão, Tua and Tinhela form the boundaries of this municipality. The Alijó Cooperative Vineyard, which produces Douro DOC, Moscatel Wine, Port Wine and Sparkling Wine, is prominent in the region's economy. Within the parishes of Alijó, in addition to the seat of the municipality, Favaios, a Wine village, and Vila do Pinhão are among the highlights.

DOLMEN OF FONTE COBERTA

AGEING CELLARS

Quinta da Avessada has the first interactive wine cellar of the Iberian Peninsula. Here is produced the famous muscatel "Favaios". It has available a wide range of activities. There is also an interactive museum about the wine and vineyard history and culture on Alto Douro, from the vine planting, through the winemaking process and till the tasting.

Luís Barros, one of the responsible for the project, reminds that "this is an investment of our family in the cultural entertainment connected with wines, taking advantage of a patrimony built along one century by five farmers' generations, to show our land, our products and our people".

→ PAGES 64/65. PANORAMIC VIEW WITH RIVER DOURO AND PINHÃO

WINE MUSEUM

QUINTA DA AVESSADA

Letter III
Douro, September 12th 1915

My Dear Wife,

Night is falling and entering the window and I am falling over my words to tell you that I will have to prolong my stay. I know that you will employ your amiable understanding, given that our cousin is unwell and needs my help here on the farm.
In your last letter, you told me that your sister had moved there so that you do not feel so alone, so I'm counting on her good nature and endless appetite to keep you occupied. I hope that you have followed the advice I sent you and that now our cat Dennis is fully recovered.
Before the darkness decides to enter the room, without asking for permission, allow me to tell you the most pleasant news, as I know that your will be as amazed as I was. One of the most intriguing aspects of the harvests is all that happens in the press (a kind of very large tank made of granite). After the press is filled with grapes, twenty men roll up their clothes, wash their feet and enter in two rows, arm in arm. Then, they start to walk backwards

The Embrace that Narrows Distance

and forwards. The aim of this ceremony is to ensure the equal crushing of all the grapes. Therefore these men raise their feet as high as they can in a certain rhythm that allows the must to ferment. Later, the row is broken up, and without stopping to lift their feet at the same pace, they dance in couples. Outside the press, there is a man with a rod to encourage the "treaders", and another group of twenty who sing and dance to the sound of instruments, such as the drum, triangle and concertina, waiting for their turn to enter (around four hours later).

My dear, for sure you would never recall such a ceremony, when you drink your goblet of Port Wine, but believe me that everybody says that the more you move inside the press, and the greater your joy, the better the wine will be.

I am now going to have supper, to later cover myself with these white sheets which remind me of the whiteness of your face that i so desperately miss.

I anxiously await your news.
From your homesick husband

Steven Naylor

Fictional text based on a true story

PINHÃO BRIDGE IN DOURO RIVER

TILE PANEL IN THE TRAIN STATION

Vila do Pinhão, located in an area classified by Unesco as World Heritage, right in the heart of the Alto Douro, was one of the most emblematic trading posts for transporting Port Wine to Gaia by Rabelo boat. Pinhão train station, which was built in the 19th century, and which encouraged the development of the village, is one of the most beautiful stations in the country, and boasts one of the best collections of Portuguese tiles. Scenes from daily life related to wine culture and economy are depicted on the tile panels. Pinhão, with its magnificent landscapes and farms on the banks of the River Douro, together with its cuisine, has become one of the most highly recommended destinations in Douro.

TRAIN STATION

A PAIR OF OXEN CROSSING THE DOURO RIVER NEAR PINHÃO (BEGINNING OF THE 20TH CENTURY)

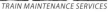
TRAIN MAINTENANCE SERVICES

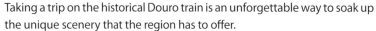

Taking a trip on the historical Douro train is an unforgettable way to soak up the unique scenery that the region has to offer.

The trip takes place every Saturday from May to October, in a 20th century steam locomotive. Over the 28ml that separate the stations of Régua and Tua, the train follows the meandering river, just metres from its edge, allowing you to enjoy extraordinary views of the hills, the farms and their vineyards.

The Douro Line was finished with the connection to Spain in 1887. At the end of the last century, the connection to Spain, and that between Pocinho and Barca de Alva, were discontinued. Now, only the link between Porto and Pocinho is active.

During the trip, you can taste Port Wine with a regional cake, accompanied by regional music and songs.

TRAIN AT THE BRIDGE OVER THE TUA RIVER JUNCTION WITH THE DOURO RIVER

HISTORICAL TRAIN AT PINHÃO'S TRAIN STATION

CASA DA QUINTA

QUINTA VELHA

DONA CLARA TERRACE

MUSIC ROOM

Quinta da Romaneira was recently acquired and restructured by foreign investors, who transformed this ancient villa into a luxury tourism complex. With 400 hectares that extend all the way to the River Douro, Quinta da Romaneira's exquisite and distinctive decoration surprises, as does the pleasantness and professionalism of its staff. The stocks of Douro wines at Quinta da Romaneira are especially earmarked for consumption in the house restaurant, which enjoys magnificent views. By staying at this farm you can choose to go to the pool, the solarium with view to the Douro River, the chocolate store, the spa or the library. You can also participate in wine tastings, boat trips and all-terrain vehicle rides.

WINTER GARDEN OF QUINTA VELHA

PANORAMIC VIEW OF PRAÇA DA REPÚBLICA (SQUARE)

Located at the heart of the Cima Corgo, the village of São João da Pesqueira enjoys magnificent landscapes, with its shale hills snaked by terraced planted with vines. It boasts one of the best views over the River Douro, such as the Viewpoint of São Salvador do Mundo, and has a vast cultural and architectural heritage. It is one of the municipalities with the largest production of Port Wine, and has one of the most extensive areas classified by UNESCO as Word Heritage. Walk around the historical centre of the village, taste its cuisine and seek out memorable landscapes.

PRAÇA DA RÉPUBLICA (SQUARE)

TILE PANEL OF THE CHAPEL

MUSEUM

CASA DO CABO

LANDSCAPE VIEWED FROM QUINTA DAS CARVALHAS

Quinta das Carvalhas, located on the Douro hillsides, is mentioned as being the "jewel in the crown" of its owner - Real Companhia Velha. The oldest reference to this farm, considered one of the biggest of the region, dates from 1759.

Real Companhia Velha organises tours with wine tastings included. This company was established in 1756, by Royal Charter of the King D. José I, and was formed by the most important farmers of Alto Douro, aiming to "support the vineyard cultivation, keeping the production at its natural purity". It was also assigned with the so-called Pombaline Demarcation of Douro region, being the Feitoria do Douro wine region the oldest demarcated and regulated wine region of the world.

→ *PAGES. 80 / 81. FRUIT SELLER, CAFÉ TEIXEIRA, ROGAS, TYPICAL BARBERSHOP*   *QUINTA DAS CARVALHAS*

PORCA DE MURÇA

The origins of Murça predate the founding of Portuguese nationality, as various archaeological remnants prove, beginning with the Palheiros fortified hill town, around five thousand years old. The best known monument in the village is the Porca de Murça, around which legends have grown up. It is a zoomorphic statue representing a wild hog, a Verraco, a fertility symbol among the proto-historic peoples. To get to know the cultural heritage of the municipality, it is possible to choose various tourist routes, as well as take the opportunity to taste the local cuisine, namely the famous cupcakes and "toucinho do céu" desserts, which are made from squash, almonds and egg yolks.

PILLORY   *ROTUNDA DA OLIVEIRA (ROUNDABOUT)*

The doors were green and the windowpanes, darkened by time, hardly allowed what was happening inside to be seen. However, whenever curiosity got the better of me, I could always be found peeking through one of the windows.

Inside, below a lamp that illuminated the souls more than the walls, a chair would become a throne for the men who sat there, one at a time, to see their beard being shaved and, once in a while, their hair being cut, on that ancient mirror in which their reflection could hardly be discerned. The walls were lined with newspapers, photographs, posters and calendars from various periods. Three stools on the right provided a place for those who were chattering while they waited in the hope that the razor would do its work without leaving any cuts.

I liked to hear the laughter of the men and the lads. Sometimes, my father took out a bottle of Port Wine that he kept as his most precious possession inside one of the cupboards beside the chair. When this happened, a spontaneous exchange of toasts occurred with small goblets, and the laughter doubled in intensity.

On one of these days on which I was trying to uncover what was happening inside, I realised that there was no activity, because it was harvest time. My father ended up sleeping in the chair where he usually never sat. Without

The Embrace of the Wine

him noticing, I opened one of the doors and played with all the utensils there, except the razor. I carefully observed the photographs and there was one of a certain Mr. Naylor, who had become a friend of my grandfather's, also a barber, another of a cooper, whose name I cannot recall, but who had offered a cask hand made by him to his friend from Douro who visited at least once a year. They were just photographs of men that had been there to trim their beards and taste the wine. As it wasn't school time, and I didn't have anything else to do, I decided to comb his hair very slowly and I thought, at that time, that it looked much better with one of my hair slides. As soon as I finished styling it, I exited quietly and left him to continue his restful sleep, which was well deserved.

This innocent act was the subject of much laughter wherever my father went, with his wooden box, to go to some customers' houses to shave them in the early evening. Without understanding the reason for so much mirth, my father joined in the laughter until the time at which he raised his hand to his head and soon realised what was going on. As soon as he arrived back at the barber's shop, he summoned me, and, filled with fear of how he could react towards me, in the end I received from his hands my first goblet of Port Wine, whose flavour was and always will be timeless, just like its presence in our lives.

Fictional text based on a true story

A SHEPHERD AND HIS FLOCK

DOLMEN OF ZEDES

ANSIÃES CASTLE

Carrazeda de Ansiães has its origins in the old village of Ansiães, from which remain ruins of the castle, the houses and the Roman churches of São Salvador and São João. It is worth visiting the villages in the municipality, such as Vilarinho da Castanheira, Linhares and others. You can also appreciate some treasures of the archaeological heritage of the region, such as the Zedes dolmen and Ansiães castle. The municipality's economy is still essentially rural. In addition to the importance of wine-growing, the production of olive oil and fruit is of particular importance. Here and there, there are craft activities, such as sacred sculptures in wood, basket weaving and cooperage. The importance of the Tua railway in terms of heritage is also notable, being a daring work of engineering from the 19th century.

ROMAN FOUNTAIN

OLIVE TREE GROVE

MAIN CHURCH

Vila Flor has traces of Bronze Age settlement, and everywhere there are remnants of hill fort ruins and Roman buildings. King D. Dinis gave the region the name Vila Flor (Flower Village) because he found it florid and pretty, and ordered walls to be built around the city, one of the five original arched gates remaining until today. The primary sector is prominent in the regional economy, with wine production, olive oil, almonds and various fruits. Vila Flor has one of the best and most popular campsites in the northern inland area of the country, within the Peneiredo Tourism Complex. In terms of scenery, Monte de Nossa Senhora da Lapa is of particular importance.

D. DINIS ARCH

NUMÃO CASTLE

Vila Nova de Foz Côa is situated in an area where the climate is hot enough to enable the cultivation of fig, olive, orange and almond trees. The river Douro and the Côa Valley mark their imposing presence in the region. The "Rota dos Miradouros de Foz Côa" (The "Foz Côa Viewpoints Route") affords silent moments in communion with Nature while enjoying the scenery of the wine-producing area, as well as the almonds in blossom and the castles. The latter have served as both lookouts and defences, and you can visit the castles at Numão, Castelo Melhor and Castelo Velho. The one at Castelo Melhor was constructed between the 9th and 10th centuries. Seen from a distance it looks like a king's crown.

FREIXO DE NUMÃO

CASTELO MELHOR

RURAL LANDSCAPE IN NUMÃO

→ PAGES. 88/89 *BLOSSOMING ALMOND TREE IN ALMENDRA, V. N. DE FOZ CÔA*

MUSEU DO CÔA

The name Foz Côa is associated with the rock art of the Upper Palaeolithic Period in the valleys of the Côa and Douro rivers. They were officially discovered in 1995, during the construction of the Côa dam. The Côa Valley has been classified as a national monument, as it contains the largest Upper Palaeolithic outdoor museum in the world and is a site considered as a World Cultural Heritage Site by UNESCO.

Visits to the rock art are subject to prior registration. They are organized into three sections: Canada do Inferno (from Vila Nova de Foz Côa), Penascosa (from Castelo Melhor) and Ribeira dos Piscos (from Muxagata).

The Côa Museum, harmoniously merged into the landscape, provides a detailed summary of the extensive period of rock art to be found in the Côa Valley Archaeological Park. The museum grew out of a project designed by the architects Camilo Rebelo and Tiago Pimentel. During a visit to it, you can learn about this valuable heritage thanks to the use of new technologies. The museum, which opened in 2010, is surrounded by two UNESCO World Cultural Heritage Sites: The Douro Wine Region and the Côa Valley. So far over 26 km of engravings have been discovered, i.e. over 1000 examples of rock art, but only 3 of the 66 sites containing engravings can be visited. This art stems from the time when homo sapiens came to Europe. The Upper Palaeolithic representations in the Côa Valley show large-sized wild animals which were hunted.

ROCK ART FROM PENASCOSA PARK

QUINTA DO VESÚVIO

HARVEST

Quinta do Vesúvio, established on the south bank of the River Douro, boasts a unique landscape within Douro Superior. The farm has an area of 325 ha, with plantations of vineyards, olives, almonds, oranges and honey production. Quinta do Vesúvio maintains the tradition of grape treading in shale presses. This was D. Antónia's large farm, where she, and before her, her uncle and her husband, made the largest investments of the time. In 1989, Quinta do Vesúvio was bought by the Symington family, which already plays a role on the Port Wine production for over a century.

CELLAR

GRAPE TREADING

VIEW OVER THE DOURO RIVER AT QUINTA DO VESÚVIO

TYPICAL HOUSES

MAIN CHURCH

DETAIL OF THE CHURCH

TYPICAL HOUSE

PHILIPPINE FOUNTAIN

The current village of Torre de Moncorvo was founded by King D. Dinis, who ordered the construction of the castle, some remnants of whose structure still exist. In relation to architectural heritage, the 17th century church stands out, the largest of the parish churches in the Trás-os-Montes area. In the whole village, there are several chapels, fountains and manor houses that deserve your attention.

The River Sabor flows through the municipality, a tributary of the River Douro considered one of the truly wild rivers in Europe with an ecosystem harbouring a wide variety of mammals, birds and flora. Also in the municipality is the Serra do Reboredo, which has the largest white oak forest in Europe.

Alfândega da Fé

Alfândega da Fé is a village that makes part of the municipality of Bragança. Its name is related to Moorish origins, when they were in the region during the 8th century.

The origin of the name 'Alfandagh' means 'inn'. The village and the surrounding areas have mountains, high plains, and the landscape is full of cherry trees, almond trees, olive trees and vineyards.

Visit the Clock Tower and taste the delicious cherries. Take a rest at the beautiful Hotel & Spa Alfândega da Fé.

VILARELHOS, SALGUEIRO DAM

CLOCK TOWER

Mirandela

In the municipality of Mirandela one can find evidence of its pre-historic origins and of the ancient people who explored different metals in the area.

We recommend a visit to the Old Bridge, the Távora Palace, the Count of Vinhais Manor and the Pillories of Frechas da Torre de Dona Chama, each of which forms part of Mirandela's heritage. The River Tua banks and beautiful stretch of water offer all kinds of watersports and outdoor tourist activities and reflect the image of a city brought to life. In Mirandela you can also find the "lagares", the traditional stone tanks used to squash grapes, and "engenhos de água", water deposits, demonstrating the importance of olive oil to this region. One highlight of Mirandela's cuisine is the "alheiras", traditional smoked sausage, and the "folar de carne", a type of meat roll.

OLD BRIDGE, MIRANDELA

MARIALVA CASTLE

CITY COUNCIL

The city of Mêda is located between the Beirão high plain and Alto Douro, and the varied landscape alternates between granite mountains, almond trees in bloom, olive groves and pines. Among the various locations, the castle and Roman bridge in Longroiva, Ranhados castle and the Historical Village of Marialva are of particular interest. In relation to the economy of the municipality, wine-growing and the Adega Cooperativa da Mêda, the production of chestnuts, almonds and olive oil are prominent.

CASTLE OF LONGROIVA

→ PAGE 100/101 *LANDSCAPES OF DOURO RIVER IN UPPER DOURO*

$\mathcal{I}$ rise before the sun. It is always this way in August and September. There is no time for the children and the house is empty. The green door stays closed awaiting other days on which life is reborn inside.

I count on my grandmother's help to deal with the children. I follow the path to the farm with my mother. I did not forget the scissors, or the headscarf. This sun is scalding and scorching.

My mother always comes dressed in black, and brings a straw hat to cover her sad eyes, ever since my father left in another harvest that will always remain in our memories. The words are few and raw, but her steps are firm and vigorous, and it is not easy keeping up with her.

The Embrace of the Branches

As soon as we arrive at the farm, we pick up the washed baskets. My mother always grumbles because they are not wicker, but those are the rules and we must adapt to them.

Just after we begin to cut the bunches of grapes, all the sorrow drains away to the banks of the River Douro, which observes us attentively. The azure of the sky welcomes us with firmness and the vine leaves embrace us fearlessly. The grape juice that runs through our hands, leaving its mark on our skin, brings us the joy to sing.
Only we can understand these branches that we cut and this land that we tread. We speak of love with the vineyards. We sing of hope, even when it is the silence that wants to burst from our throats. We sing of joy "until the baskets have been washed."

Fictional text based on a true story

TYPICAL HOUSE

MAIN CHURCH

PILLORY

The village of Barcos is based in the municipality of Tabuaço, and dates back to the Bronze Age. You cannot miss a visit to the 12th century Main Church which has a gilded altar and a painted ceiling, and to the shrine of Santa Maria de Sabroso. Several houses with coat of arms illustrating the economic importance of the village in terms of wine production are scattered around the parish.

TYPICAL STREET OF BARCOS

GENERAL VIEW OF FAVAIOS

COOPERATIVE WINERY

The wine village of Favaios, which is thought to have been inhabited by the Romans in the 1st and 2nd centuries, lent its name to its most renowned product, the Moscatel de Favaios, produced at the Adega Cooperativa.
In addition to the renowned Moscatel, this parish of Alijó is known for producing the best bread in the region, produced in wood-burning ovens, its traditional bakeries being well worth a visit.

FAVAIOS BREAD

SCHIST HOUSE

PILLORY

TYPICAL HOUSES OF BARCOS

The village of Provesende is located in the municipality of Sabrosa, in a high region of Douro that slopes down a valley to the village of Pinhão. The origins of Provesende have been lost in time. According to legend, it was associated with a Moorish settlement, reconquered by the Christians. Since the Middle Ages, it has been the seat of a municipality and boasts, even today, signs of former nobility and economic importance, with eleven stately homes.

ARCHITECTURAL DETAIL FROM THE VILLAGE

QUELHO DE SALZEDAS

MONASTERY OF SANTA MARIA DE SALZEDAS (CLOISTERS)

MONASTERY (FAÇADE)

Salzedas dates back to the 12th century, when the Cistercian Monastery of Santa Maria de Salzedas was built. This monastery, which is a national monument, became one of the richest, largest and most important Portuguese monasteries, and had a notable library. One of the attractions of the village is the collection of houses and streets called "Quelho de Salzedas." We also recommend visiting the viewpoints and places of worship in Santa Bárbara and Lady of Mercy, as well as the Romanesque bridge of Vila Pouca.

FORTIFIED BRIDGE OF UCANHA OVER VAROSA RIVER

INTERIOR OF THE TOWER'S UPPER FLOOR

Belonging to the municipality of Tarouca, the village of Ucanha is the oldest "Village" in the surrounding areas, and has vestiges of the presence of the Romans throughout sections of a road that leads to Lamego. The River Varosa flows through the village, a tributary of the Douro, and its main attraction is the Fortified Bridge, dating from 1465, in gothic style. This is a rare structure in Portugal, once used to collect tolls for passing through the village belonging to the protectorate of Salzedas. You should also not miss the Caves de Murganheira to taste their famous sparkling wine.

DETAILS FROM THE TYPICAL HOUSES OF UCANHA

MURGANHEIRA WINE CELLARS

HOUSES AT THE VISCONDE LÓ FERREIRA SQUARE

HOUSES AT TREVÕES

Trevões is the Wine-growing Village of the municipality of S. João da Pesqueira and has a strong religious culture, illustrated by the number of chapels and hermitages, of which the Capela de Nossa Senhora da Conceição is the best known.

The Ethnographic Museum of Trevões is worth visiting, given that there you can get to know the culture, work and way of life of the village's inhabitants. In Trevões, the famous wild boar hunts, which take place in the winter months, are also renowned.

CHAPEL OF NOSSA SENHORA DA CONCEIÇÃO

International Douro Natural Park was classified as such in 1998, and extends along the cliffs of the Rivers Douro and Águeda, on the border with Spain. It is a park with very particular characteristics, and contains rich fauna and flora that, in Portugal, can only be found in this region, some species even being endemic. The River Douro enters our country through the Mirandês Plateau between abrupt and tortuous cliffs that tear and break its soft nuances. Some of these cliffs are between 164 and 274 yd high and, were it not for the dams, the river would continue to flow through these gorges dramatically and violently. This sinuous path almost 93 mi in length starts at an average altitude of 766 yd, dropping to 164 yd in Barca d'Alva, where the river starts to calm down and flow more gently. The park is the habitat of species of bird such as the Golden Eagle, the Black Stork, the Egyptian Vulture, Bonelli's Eagle and the Peregrine Falcon. Mammals include the Wolf, the Pyrenean Desman, the Common Bent-wing Bat, Cabrera's Vole, the Otter, the Wildcat, etc. Among flora, there is the holm oak, the juniper, the ash, the European nettle tree, the olive tree, the oak and the park's endemic flower: the *paeonia broteri*.

VIEWPOINT AT CASTRO DE VALE DA ÁGUIA, MIRANDA DO DOURO

PENEDO DURÃO, FREIXO DE ESPADA À CINTA

AERIAL VIEW OF BARCA D'ALVA

MIRANDÊS DONKEY AND LOCAL INHABITANT

VIEWPOINT IN S. JOÃO DAS ARRIBAS, MIRANDA DO DOURO ↑ ↗

$\mathscr{I}$t was a Saturday afternoon, one of those on which the desert grows in the heart of those who have little time left to live and words become the most precious inheritance that can be passed down.

The words were music that enchanted that granddaughter, so surprised to hear her grandmother speaking in a tone that she couldn't understand. Normally she spoke about matters that did not interest her, and she barely listened, but this time, as they followed the path, just the two of them, side by side, it seemed that her grandmother's senses were more keen than ever. They had been to Sabrosa to spend the weekend with their parents and younger sister.

The invitation to go for a walk didn't seem very attractive, but as soon as the phrases addressed to her began to fall from her grandmother's lips, her eyes widened with surprise. It was thus that, for the first time, she heard about her great-grandfather, the cooper, and the role, so difficult, that he performed with the same love with which he dedicated himself to his paintings. She was fifteen, and she discovered at that moment that the moon,

The Embrace of the Moon

her source of inspiration, actually did have magic powers. Her grandmother explained to her that it was between October and December that the trees that barrel staves were based on were cut down. They had to be felled in the dim light of the moon, because then the wood had its blood closed. The third quarter, according to her grandfather, was the best moon to cut the oak without it bleeding. The granddaughter started reflecting on what blood that was, but resisted the temptation to interrupt her grandmother.

Thus, with her gaze held high, the elderly lady continued talking about the workshop where her father used to work in Vila Nova de Gaia and all the care he took in looking after the wood, from cutting to the time at which the barrel was ready to be delivered to a cellar owner. It was a lengthy process that required patience and perfectionism. Any fault could mean an irreparable loss of the wine that would be put inside it to mature.
For the granddaughter, the perfection would always reside in that afternoon, which would always remain the most precious legacy in her heart.

Fictional text based on a true story

GENERAL VIEW OF CASTELO RODRIGO

PORTA DO SOL

The municipality of Figueira de Castelo Rodrigo has a magnificent landscape surrounded by the rivers Côa and the Rivers Águeda and Douro, in the International Douro Natural Park. The following locations are worthy of mention: the parish of Castelo Rodrigo and Barca De Alva, in the parish of Escalhão. Castelo Rodrigo is a medieval fortified Historical Village, located at an altitude of 897yd, and its surrounding views are fantastic.

Barca D'Alva, which borders Spain, was once an important customs post and made the rail connection between Porto and the rest of Europe, trough Salamanca.

In the entire municipality, during the months of February and March, the landscapes are filled with white and pink from the blossoming almond trees.

PAGE 117 → (from up to the right)

01- BELL TOWER

02- TYPICAL HOUSE

03- MAIN CHURCH

04- CASTELO RODRIGO

VIEW OF PENEDO DURÃO

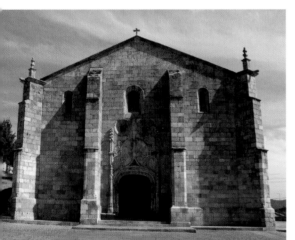

MAIN CHURCH

"TORRE DO GALO"

Freixo de Espada à Cinta is a municipality located in the centre of the International Douro Natural Park.

The origins of the village date back to pre-Roman times, and its lands were successively conquered by peoples of different origins. We recommend a visit to the Heptagonal Tower, the Manueline Main Church, the village Pillory and a walk around the typical streets of the historical quarter. The tradition of the silk remains on the municipality, with ancestral processes of spinning and weaving. As for the landscape that the municipality offers, the magnificent viewpoints of Penedo Durão, Carrascalinho, Colado das Alminhas and Cruzinhas are particularly noteworthy. This municipality becomes more florid at the end of winter, with its blossoming almond trees.

MOGADOURO CASTLE

MAIN CHURCH

Mogadouro is an old village, which was populated by prehistoric peoples. It is located at the beginning of the Transmontano high plain, and part of the municipality falls within the International Douro Natural Park. Its natural landscape also covers Vale do Sabor. In the months of February and March, the almond trees bloom and embellish the terraces of the village. You should visit Mogadouro Castle Tower and Penas Róias Castle.

CLOCK TOWER

MAIN CHURCH

SCULPTURE BY ANTÓNIO NOBRE: TRADITIONAL COSTUMES FROM MIRANDA DO DOURO

The origins of Miranda do Douro date back a long way, and it progressively became the most important fortified town in Trás-os-Montes. The municipality possesses a valuable cultural heritage spread over the different parishes, which continue to preserve part of their culture and popular traditions. On the Miranda high plain, winter solstice festivals are still celebrated today, with rituals of profound mythological significance. In 1998, Mirandese officially became Portugal's second language. A large part of the municipality lives off agriculture and grazing, and the breeds Bovina Mirandesa, Churra Galega Mirandesa, Asinina Mirandesa and Cão de Gado Transmontano are native to the region. The spectacular cliffs of International Douro Natural Park are a highlight among the landscapes of the Mirandese plateau.

PAGE 121 → (from up to the right)

01- PANORAMIC VIEW OF MIRANDA

02- EPISCOPAL PALACE

03- PAULITEIROS DE MIRANDA

MIRANDÊS DONKEY | PICTURE OF A SHEPHERD, A "TRANSMONTANO" CATTLE DOG AND THE FLOCK, IN IFANES, MIRANDA DO DOURO

S. JOÃO DE TAROUCA CHURCH

Tarouca

Tarouca falls in the Vale of Varosa region and its landscape is diverse and filled with olive groves, vineyards, orchards of apple and pear trees, and in May we can observe and feel the sweet aroma of the sambucus flower. Tarouca is the municipality with the largest production of berries of this aromatic plant. Part of the municipality belongs to the Demarcated Wine-growing Region of Távora-Varosa. You should not miss the opportunity to visit the Church of São Pedro de Tarouca, the Monastery of São João de Tarouca and the Wine-growing villages of Ucanha and Salzedas.

BRIDGE OVER VAROSA RIVER

Moimenta da Beira

The first evidences of settlement of the municipality of Moimenta da Beira are located on the Necrópole Megalíca da Nave. There are also many remnants of the presence of the Romans. In the centre of the Village, the Largo das Fontainhas, the S. João Fountain and the Casa da Moimenta are of particular importance. Part of the municipality falls within the Demarcated Wine-growing Region of Távora-Varosa, a region where white wine, red wine and sparkling wine is produced. Allow yourself to be enchanted by the typical Beira landscapes and indulge in the regional cuisine.

TYPICAL GRANARY

GUEST HOUSE

CARVALHOS' MANOR-HOUSE

Sernancelhe

The economy of Sernancelhe is centred on agricultural activity, essentially the production of wine, apples and chestnuts. The landscape of the municipality is diverse, with high plains and mountains, woods and thickets, ravines and valleys and the Távora reservoir. You may visit the historical villages of Fonte Arcada, Ferreirim and Freixinho. In the seat of the municipality, you may enjoy the religious architecture. The Portuguese writer Aquilino Ribeiro (1885-1963) was born in Tabosa do Carregal.

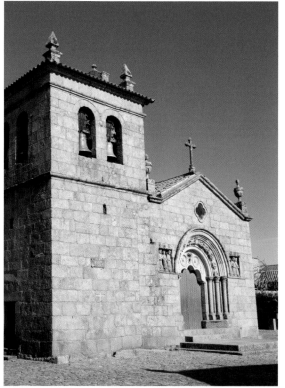

MAIN CHURCH

Penedono

The municipality of Penedono plays host to several monuments and vestiges which testify its antiquity and historical richness. From prehistoric times, the Capela de Nossa Senhora do Monte dolmen, which is a National Monument, is of particular importance. Of the architectural heritage, the Pillories of Penedono and Souto, the Churches of São Salvador, Freixos Manor-House and the former Municipality Hall building are worthy of mention. We strongly advise you to visit Penedono Castle, classified as a National Monument, which has the peculiarity of being a pentagonal castle. The municipality is one of the largest producers of chestnuts, exporting much of this product.

PENEDONO CASTLE

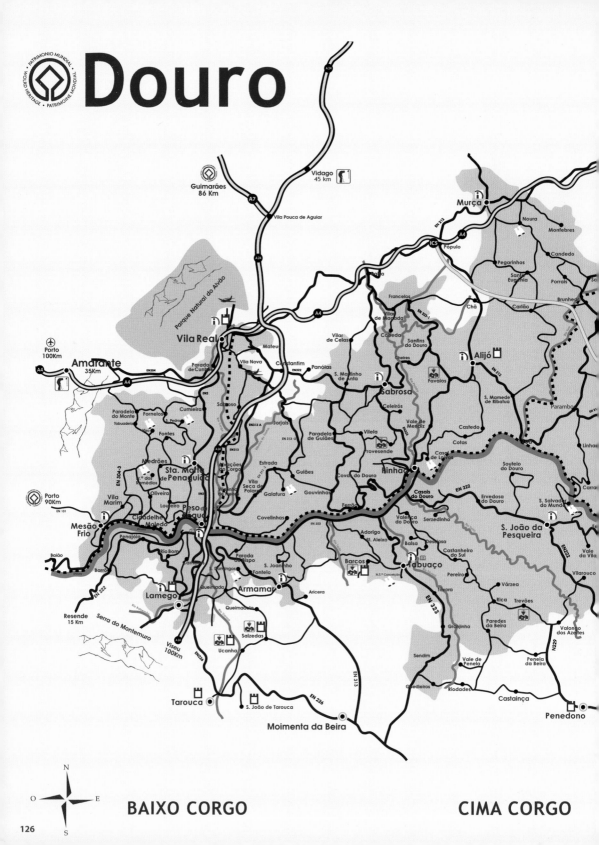

Douro

PATRIMONIO MUNDIAL · WORLD HERITAGE · PATRIMOINE MONDIAL

Guimarães 86 Km

Vidago 45 km

Vila Pouca de Aguiar

Porto 100Km

Amarante 35Km

Vila Real

Murça

Noura

Monfebres

Pópulo

Candedo

Pegarinhos

Santa Eugénia

Porrais

Brunhega

Francelos

Chã

Carlão

Vilar de Maçada

Parada de Cunha

Vila Nova

Mateus

Constantim

Vilar de Celas

Cabeda

Sanfins do Douro

Panóias

S. Martinho de Anta

Cheires

Alijó

Paradela do Monte

Fornelos

Cumieira

Pedregal

Sabroso

Sabrosa

Favaios

S. Mamede de Ribatua

Parambo

Tobuadela

Fontes

EN313 A

Jorjais

Celeirós

Vale de Mendiz

Castedo

Linhar

Porto 90Km

Medrões

Nações do Corgo

EN313

Paradela de Guiães

Estrada

Vilela

Provesende

Cotas

Soutelo do Douro

Carra

STA. MARTA de Penaguião

Sra. dos Remedios

Oliveira

Loureiro

Peso da Régua

Vila Seca de Poiares

Galafura

Guiães

Cova do Douro

Pinhão

Casa de Loivos

Casais do Douro

S. Salvador do Mundo

Ervedosa do Douro

S. João da Pesqueira

Vila Marim

Mesão Frio

Cidadelhe Moledo

Penajoia

Covelinhas

Ferrão

Valença do Douro

Serzedinho

Desposa

Castanheiro do Sul

Vale da Vila

Resende 15 km

Baião

Barra

Rio Bom

Domingos

Parada do Bispo

S. Joaninho

Adorigo

St. Aleixo

Balsa

Tabuaço

Pereiro

Vilarouco

Lamego

Armamar

Aricera

Barcos

N.ª Conceição

Távora

Rica

Trevões

Queimadela

Serra do Montemuro

Queimada

Salzedas

Ucanha

Sendim

Granjinha

Valongo dos Azeites

Vale de Penela

Penela da Beira

Viseu 100Km

Tarouca

S. João de Tarouca

EN 226

Galedeiros

Riodades

Castainça

Penedono

Moimenta da Beira

N O E S

BAIXO CORGO

CIMA CORGO

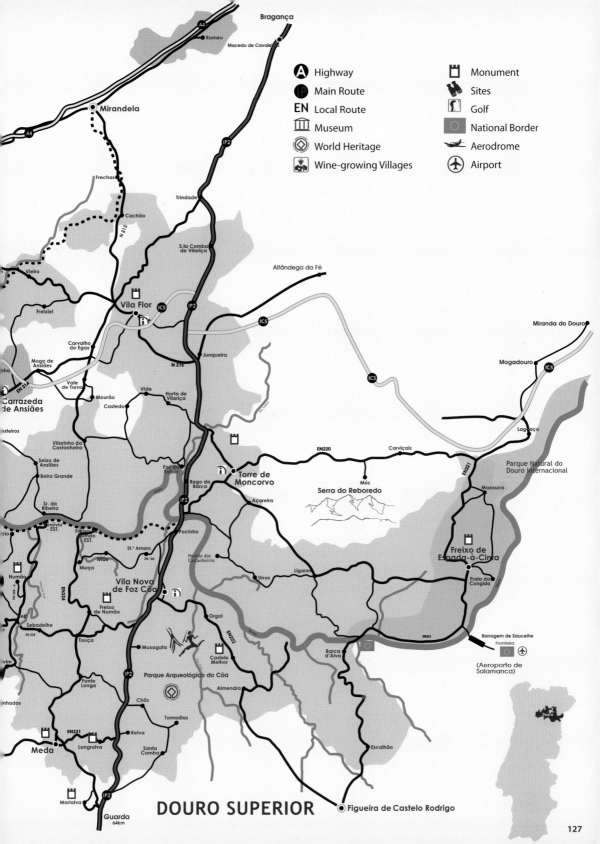

Bragança

Romeu
A4
Macedo de Cavaleiros

Mirandela
A4
Frechas
IP2
Cachão
N 213
Trindade

S.ta Comba
de Vilariça

Alfândega da Fé

Miranda do Douro

Vieiro
Vila Flor
IC5
IP2
IC5
Mogadouro
IC5

Freixiel
Carvalho
do Egas
Junqueira
N 215

Mogo de
Ansiães
Vale
de Torno
Mourão
Vide
Horta de
Vilariça
IC5
Lagoaça

Carrazeda
de Ansiães
Castedo
EN 214

Parque Natural do
Douro Internacional

esteiros
Vilarinho da
Castanheira
EN220
Carviçais
Mazouco

Seixo de
Ansiães
Foz do
Sabor
Mós
EN221

Beira Grande
Rego da
Barca
Torre de
Moncorvo
Serra do Reboredo

Sr. da
Ribeira
Açoreira
Freixo de
Espada-à-Cinta

súvio
EST.
Freixo
?mão
EST.
Pocinho
IP2
Praia da
Congida

Numão
St.º Amaro
EN 102
Perelo dos
Castanheiros
Ligares
Urros

Mós
Murça
EN324
Vila Nova
de Foz Côa
Freixo
de Numão
Orgal
EN222
Barragem de Saucelhe
Fronteira

Sebadelhe
EN 222
Touça
Muxagata
Castelo
Melhor
Barca
d'Alva
EN221
(Aeroporto de
Salamanca)

vim
IP2
Fonte
Longa
Parque Arqueológico do Côa
Almendra

nhados
Chãs

Tomadias

Meda
EN331
Longroiva
Relva
Santa
Comba
Escalhão

Marialva
IP2

Guarda
64km

Douro

DOURO SUPERIOR

Figueira de Castelo Rodrigo

Legend:
Ⓐ Highway
🅿 Main Route
EN Local Route
🏛 Museum
◎ World Heritage
👥 Wine-growing Villages
🏰 Monument
🔭 Sites
⛳ Golf
National Border
✈ Aerodrome
✈ Airport

EDITORIAL PROJECT:
Objecto Anónimo, Lda.

AUTHORSHIP:
Pedro Veloso, Susana Fonseca, Sérgio Fonseca

GRAPHIC DESIGN / PHOTOGRAPHY:
Pedro Veloso, Sérgio Fonseca

TEXT EDITING AND COORDINATION / CREATIVE TEXTS:
Susana Fonseca

Texts:
Susana Fonseca, Pedro Veloso

TRANSLATION:
Eurologos - Porto / Certas Palavras, Susana Santos

SPECIAL THANKS TO:
Museu do Douro, Instituto dos Vinhos do Douro e Porto, Porto Cálem, Quinta da Pacheca, Quinta das Carvalhas, Quinta do Panascal, Quinta do Seixo, Quinta da Avessada, Quinta do Côtto, Solar da Rede, Casa de Mateus, Quinta do Vallado, Quinta do Portal, Quinta Nova de Nossa Sra. do Carmo, Quinta da Romaneira, Quinta do Vesúvio, Associação Transumância e Natureza, Paula Cerqueira, Sandra Bandeira, Jorge Pópulo, and especially to Gaspar Martins Pereira.

PHOTOGRAPHY CREDITS:
Photos from the collection of the Instituto dos Vinhos do Douro e do Porto, I. P., pages 12, 16, 17, 20
Photos from the collection of the Instituto dos Vinhos do Douro e do Porto, I. P., taken by de Álvaro Cardoso de Azevedo (Casa Alvão) pages 21, 69, 82, 83
IPTM - Instituto Portuário e dos Transportes Marinhos, pages 112 (2)
Rui Pires, pages 75 (2)
João Cosme, pages 114 (2), 115
Fernando Romão, pages 114 (3)
Museu do Douro, pages 18, 19

LITERARY CREDITS:
Gaspar Martins Pereira, Introduction pages 5-6

PRINTING:
Norprint

THIRD EDITION (revised and updated):
February- 2014
© Objecto Anónimo, Lda.

ALSO AVAILABLE IN THE FOLLOWING LANGUAGES:
Portuguese, French, Spanish and German

COLLECTION JOURNEYS AND STORIES (other publications):
Portugal, Lisbon, Porto and Northern Portugal

Maia, Portugal
info@objectoanonimo.com

ISBN 978-989-8256-07-2
Depósito Legal 310728/10